Cheapside Afterlife

poems by

George Rawlins

With an Afterword by Josh Mcloughlin

LONGLEAF PRESS

Fayetteville, North Carolina

Copyright © 2021, 2024 by George Rawlins

Afterword © 2022 by Josh Mcloughlin

All rights reserved.

Printed in the United States of America

Library of Congress Catalog Data:

Rawlins, George

Cheapside Afterlife: poems.

ISBN: 978-1-7343985-9-5 (paperback)

Cover Art: "A Post-Pre-Raphaelite Complication," from *The Chatterton Conclaves* by Roger Weingarten

Book design by Crystal Simone Smith

A Shannon Ward and Roger Weingarten publication

For author inquiries or for information about permission to reproduce selections from this book contact:

Longleaf Press

Fayetteville, North Carolina

longleafpress@gmail.com

longleafpress.org

Acknowledgments

Many thanks to the editors of the following publications, who first published these poems:

Amethyst Review (UK)	"Wherein Old Tom, Bent with Age, Imagines"
Anthropocene (UK)	"From Childhood"
	"Sidewalk Screevers"
	"A Visit to Thomas Cross, Apothecary"
Chiron Review	"At Chatterton's Café, Redcliffe Way"
The Common	"Epistle to the Hangman's Mistress"
	"To Be Human"
Dreich (UK)	"Of the Immaculate Father"
	"Southwark Broadside"
	"The Word of Rowley Ripens, Briefly, into Flesh"
Ephemeral Elegies	"By Reason's Fright and Firelight"
First Literary Review-East	"How to Give Up Poetry: A Broadside"
Former People	"Dear Thomas"
Illuminations	"Impromptu Portraits, Early Spring"
	"Sadness of the Carriage"
	"Shadow of the Enlightenment"
Littoral Press (UK)	"Cabinet of Wonders"
	"Eclogue the Nth"
	"From the Sacred Texts"
	"In Which Thomas Propositions an Angel"
	"A jot of blood"
	"On Hogarth's *The Bruiser*"
The Madrigal (Ireland)	"Off *Gin Lane*, waltzing"
Modern Literature	"Ambition"
	"Essay on Composition"

	"In the Chase Near Portishead"
	"Leigh Woods Pastoral, with Uncertainty"
	"Mystery Play"
Neologism Poetry Journal	"Worlds Betwixt"
New Critique (UK)	"Indecision"
	"Quick Note to Mother"
New World Writing	"Anatomy of the Soul"
	"At Colston Hospital School"
	"By St George's Hill"
	"Essay on Knowledge"
	"Port of Call"
Nine Mile	"Every Day a Little Suicide"
	"On the Resurgence of Plague in Moscow"
	"Thomas Seeks a Patron or Lunch"
One Hand Clapping (UK)	"1770, London"
	"A Last August"
	"Red Cliffs"
	"The Resurrection of Thomas Chatterton"
Open: Journal of Arts & Letters	"Chatterton Meets Rimbaud"
	"Grub Street Parties"
Sein und Werden (UK)	"Eighteenth-Century Pastimes"

I would like to thank my mentors and readers over the years: the inimitable Wayne Dodd for great expectations, Charles Wright, James McMichael, Sharon Doubiago, David Dodd Lee, April Ossmann, and David Koehn. Most of all I would like to thank Roger Weingarten, without whose guidance, insight, and friendship this book would never have been written.

Many thanks to Shannon Ward at Longleaf Press for choosing to publish this book, and to Crystal Simone Smith for her book design. I would also like to dedicate this book to the memory of Jon Anderson, a transcendent poet and soul, and of course to the memory of Thomas Chatterton himself, who was never allowed to realize his own greatness.

~For Constance

CONTENTS

Prologue
    Cabinet of Wonders   3

Part I
    A jot of blood   7
    Southwark Broadside   8
    Essay on Knowledge   9
    Ambition   10
    At Colston Hospital School   11
    From the Sacred Texts   12
    For the Green Man   13
    Of the Immaculate Father   14
    Eighteenth-Century Pastimes   15
    Red Cliffs   16
    Mystery Play   17
    Leigh Woods Pastoral, with Uncertainty   18
    By Reason's Fright and Firelight   19
    There's no way   20

Part II
    In which we introduce Friar Rowley,
        priest, nay poet   23
    Essay on Composition   24
    The Word of Friar Rowley Ripens,
        Briefly, into Flesh   25
    By St George's Hill   26
    In the Chase Near Portishead   28
    Shadow of the Enlightenment   29
    Eclogue the Nth   30
    Indecision   31
    Impromptu Portraits, Early Spring   32
    Anatomy of the Soul   34
    Tom's Inheritance   35
    Port of Call   36
    The Old Road to London   37
    Sadness of the Carriage   38

Part III
    1770, London   41
    Sidewalk Screevers   42
    Thomas Seeks a Patron, or Lunch   43
    For the Legacy of Mister Walpole   44
    Grub Street Parties   45
    Epistle to the Hangman's Mistress   46
    The Unexpurgated   47
    On the Resurgence of Plague in Moscow   48
    Against the Princess of Wales,
        Augusta of Saxe-Gotha   49
    John Wilkes Makes His Case   50
    On Hogarth's *The Bruiser*   51
    The Philosopher's Walk   52
    How to Give Up Poetry: A Broadside   53
    Chatterton Meets Rimbaud   54

Part IV
    Quick Note to Mother   57
    Off *Gin Lane*, waltzing   58
    Mister Smart's Knowhow   59
    To Be Human   60
    A Last August   61
    Dear Thomas   62
    Every Day a Little Suicide   63
    From Childhood   64
    Worlds Betwixt   65
    A Visit to Thomas Cross, Apothecary   66
    In Which Thomas Propositions an Angel   67
    Wherein Old Tom, Bent with Age,
        Imagines   68
    The Resurrection of Thomas Chatterton   69

Epilogue
    At Chatterton's Café, Redcliffe Way   73
Notes   75
Afterword   81

He was an instance that a complete genius and a complete rogue can be formed before a man is of age.

   —Horace Walpole, from a letter to William Mason

O Chatterton! that thou wert yet alive!
Sure thou would'st spread the canvas to the gale…

   —Samuel Taylor Coleridge, from "Monody on the Death of Chatterton"

PROLOGUE

Thomas Chatterton, born 1752, was the son of the sexton at St Mary Redcliffe Church in Bristol, England. His father died before Chatterton was born, leaving his mother to provide for Thomas and his sister by sewing. Chatterton began publishing his poetry at the age of 11. At 15, in an attempt to support his mother and sister, he invented the 15th-century priest-poet Thomas Rowley, creating manuscripts on old parchment found in the church basement and selling them as authentic artifacts to local noblemen. After this initial success, he sent the poems to Horace Walpole who at first believed them to be authentic but soon detected idioms and language inconsistent with the conventions of the 15th century. Walpole then rejected and scorned Chatterton, taking no notice of the brilliance of his invention. Chatterton left for London where he wrote political treatises and pornographic poems ridiculing politicians of the day and frequented the demimonde. In 1770, at age 17, unable to sell his writing and thinking himself a failure, Chatterton was found dead in his room, poisoned with arsenic by suicide or accidental overdose. Thirty years after his death, Chatterton was celebrated by the Romantics—including Coleridge, Wordsworth, and Shelley—as the precursor and epitome of Romanticism.

> To celebrate the Day;
> The God from whom Creation sprung
> Shall animate my grateful Tongue;
> From him I'll catch the Lay!
>
> —Thomas Chatterton, from "A Hymn for Christmas Day," written at age 11.

Cabinet of Wonders

Frankie Voltaire & the Enlightenments, best
cover band since Socrates rocked

Saturday night at The Royal. Why
not jitterbug the Age of Reason, booze

Euclid smooth from the grave, while this curved
earth rounds straight lines? Dizzied, aren't we

ready to retch, skirting worms that writhe
at the edge as we greet reborn

coalmen surging from the stinkdamp, appeasing
them with a trick of whisk and swabbers

over a pint quaffed from the blackest hole? Reader, please
pause to breathe the air inside our suprapubic

minds as we turn these
objects of curiosity over in our hands.

I

Vers'd by experience in the subtle art,
The myst'ries of a title I impart:
Teach the young author how to please the town,
And make the heavy drug of rhyme go down.

> —Thomas Chatterton, from "The Art of Puffing," July 1770

A jot of blood

streaked on sod, a sward loved
by moonlight to propagate a gangly

weed—once born there's naught
but counterpoint the razor's solo. Redcliffe's

belfry, a clanging lair to mourn
Father's clash with heaven; Mother's face, a shadow

cast from the clock that instead
of time measures fire. From everyday

plague, choke pears, and expectations to make
my mark, I am who cannot

be. Let's push the hours back
into shadows, disbelieve this

world, invent what's not, to spice our
humdrum tongue. Born, I go.

Southwark Broadside

Truth's serrated—slick and fickle bedfellow of
fibs—companion to ash. Sages chat 'round

the groaning press—read it here, dear proof
reader, follow the wandering screed as if hiking the royal

forest, stocked with venison for the sporting
kill, doe-eyed in his lordship's sight. Mind

the Keeper of the Kingswood's soiled cuffs and twitchy
sparrowhawk. Queen Charlotte licks

her yellow fangs, while the billowing
receipt of her infectious cargo moulders

above her slave ship harbour. Cut a sprig,
drip a bubble of mercury

into your gin. Press a dram to paper, to what makes
you—my closest conspirator—sorry.

Essay on Knowledge

As a child I must have imagined a harlequin
sexton parading his midnight rounds, lamp held

high to hex anatomists' moon-haunted
shovels shimmering with dew to light my

nightmare. When, after much grunting, they exhumed
us to be dissected in

the theatre of knowledge amongst the bleating
lambs of new science, what lesson of reason could

be mastered without tasting arsenic of the apple
seed? With what calculus did Leibnitz measure the variable

slope of suffering? How likely from the stars
portending above the cemetery where Father

lies and Newton might've staggered, over
wrought by a worm-riddled pippin, that I'll ascend?

Ambition

At twelve, Mother brought you to the meeting
house—leper's bread malformed on long

spare tables. Speeches and days of rain
drove you to almost understand what makes

men in a world that hides from its
intent just as a criminal

conceals a crime so he may save
himself. Hunger, that ingratiating parasite, has such

friends. At Custom's House, they'll trade
what comes—and if you shy, young Tom, you'll not

succeed. That rogue you fancy yourself, contrived
of youth, disappointment, and fury might

raise a hackle on the hound roused from sleep by
a morsel of beef fallen to the sawdust floor. Might not.

At Colston Hospital School

Headmaster never wanders lest starlight scorch
the nave of his alluvial noggin. The genius of his

novices, each unique as a hospital
brick, instructs the purpose of our grand

brainery. Matins of the bum brushers teach
us to sleep, bind our scalps as if tonsured by

the firmament to unrelenting ignorance. Mumble
mumps of prophets and bookkeepers, won't we

schoolboys one day drift above bluebell
automatons of St John's Burial Ground, pates shiny

as parchment upon which our lives
are etched with nails, of which we have no

say—then accept what's given, and without
asking erase our days behind?

From the Sacred Texts

Read closely these volumes pressed
from effervescent pulp of the dead, imbued

with stench of whatnot, scratched with claws
and passion, inked with pus from Beelzebub's

jugular—that poor, pathetic fiend: what's
wisdom worth if we'd rather

forget? Does passing into
irrelevance renew the romance in

us who sleep in ruins? If all must
disappear, are we not already

false? Or are we slightly
true, staring into a spoon of morning

gruel: giving nothing, tightly curled
here, newborns reaching into benippled dark?

For the Green Man

From this valley's heartless plenty, invent a life that
should have been. Free him from his imaginary

grave. Call him *Rowley*. For his
loblolly, a celestial-spiced clod; a sprig

of fur clipped from a back alley puss
to warm his pointer. Or dream a shadow

tongued Apso slobbering from the East. If
you pet its ear, you'll calm

and welcome what comes. In that gap—mouth
stretched broad as you quiver

in your hours—invent happiness, and trace the route
of crows above the meadow on their course

to a stand of lilac to violate a nest
of sparrow eggs.

Of the Immaculate Father

Sick of landscapes and poetry, what does it
take to finish a life? Ginned and bare

fisted, must we taste every
flavour to know bitterness? Can innocence

be given 'way like a Christmas toy
giraffe? What of Will Canynge, immaculate

father, pretender to the possible? How to mourn
him, who never lived? If

you cry, Tom, stand away from the grave
you imagine, away from searching

limbs that push shadows to the ground
to mix the din of your sleep, there to sell

whimsy'd wares at the sad
circus of poetmongers.

Eighteenth-Century Pastimes

Another parlour game, sirrah, or sport
of honour with blades or blunderbuss

pistols? To finger a harpsichord rescued
from fire so hot on a snow-driven

night—by our melody we know it's best
to be reborn on Venus instead of Mars. To revel

in this perfume: We may cheat at trick
taking games, spread our cards to kill

an hour with ruff-and-honours, blast
a quail or hum some Dryden—these moments feign

eternity. We won't be interrupted. The vicar's
fist on our heart pine door to give us

blessings, a sleight of hand that kindles
the beginnings that cast the shadow of our end.

Red Cliffs

Like limestone priests the Bristol
cliffs shed their burdens beneath

a deadpan heaven. What answers to this
vertigo? The only thing between you and that

narrow gap: a will to create whatever
in yourself you must, just

as the coffin maker shapes heartwood
to its end. Above your

dilemma, amid sacred
ponds and mulberries, a cloud

breaks out. Magpies call above the king's
gaunt hunter whose eye tracks a winsome

doe as she surveys
the moor, stinking with passion.

Mystery Play

Child Caliban, you sprawled over *The Compleat
Tragedies* in the mouldering

bookshop to sleep off your adolescent
jugbite. Not another afternoon of Jacob's

ladder and battledore, dodging wings
of angelic shuttlecocks. Here lies the invention

of yourself, sustained by a soup of husks
and boiled fingernails, so long before you

are the genius of the unwritten. Your ghost
quill pricking a cloud deflates

Xanadu, where Sam T. Coleridge sleeps
it off to write your name on rain

washed slate beneath a couplet to gild
the cups of heaven's poorhouse.

Leigh Woods Pastoral, with Uncertainty

There's no ushering, Tom, the hap. You treasure
her on Sunday, red bonnet bright as the flag

of a warring nation. You dream
of Africa's rivers, cool

and aimless beneath that habitual
sun, but put her off as you dream

of her, remembering Mother, her days worn
smooth by needles and fabric: you brood

over holiday joy and sadness as they lurk, twin
assassins among oak shadows that deepen this idyllic

chaos as if nature intends
all of it as you stand

midfield to call her name into this
frenetic meadow.

By Reason's Fright and Firelight

I took back my college reading list, hid
from Tom behind a crispy *Tristam*

Shandy, unread but bookmarked with a yellowed
Dear John, an opera played upon a Sahara

of pages foxed by dribbled Scotch. So much
depends on expectation, to sing

for supper, to sleep fat after long
affectations dull the edges. We'll

defend our sense of self, Tom, back
to back in the field of play, where euphemism's

our weapon of choice, and never
more will reason slouch forlorn in this study, vessels

ambered by fire, beneath smirking
hands, at two and ten, of the mantle clock.

There's no way

through, Tom, but to ride the chthonic
horse and carriage over cobbled

streets past the shops and putrid
fountains of this carnival

necropolis. Was your despair a far
cry from the Bristol

miller lamed by his father's
millstone? Or the maiden raped by Uncle

in his clock shop cellar? No
passage by inner star chart, no

dinghy to wobble through this crowded yet
lonely current, unsteady as you hold the whale

lamp above your nose
for grief to grasp the storm.

II

Here take this silver, it maie eathe thie care;
We are Goddes stewards all, nete of oure owne we bare.

—Thomas Chatterton, from the Rowley poems,
"An Excelente Balade of Charitie," 1768–1769

In which we introduce Friar Rowley, priest, nay poet

found reclining from invisible labours to savour
a Benedictine of vap'rous relics, who pens

by dawn-streaked angel's plume "An Excelente
Balade of Charitie." Whose life is not most

invention? Is not Walpole, simmering his
chunky giblets in a viscous

prose, more blanched sprite than flesh? Walpole,
who clenches wind of expired art from his lit'rate

bottle and glass into a Wedgewood jar—is
this life bearable sans beauteous

fakery? Or shall we sit and watch the exactly-who-
they-are trudge over cobble toward the colliers,

glancing heavenward as they descend, stumbling
dreamers of their own disinvention?

Essay on Composition

Sniff the Wife of Bath smoking sot
twisted in a crumbly page; browse

the stacks for sovereigns; scratch a little Will
Dugdale and Liz Cooper's *Muses Library*

where Edward the Confessor still suffers a liar's
hangover. Shake off some Samuel

Daniel melodrama with a ménage of feminine
endings, splash a double dactyl and brush

the embers off the faery into your Earl
Grey with a chastened Astrophel

or Stella. Shall we call the roll of antique
verbs for newfound verses? Shall we warp

them into newborn flesh to capture lightning
like fireflies dying in a jelly jar?

The Word of Friar Rowley Ripens, Briefly, into Flesh

Preening in your hair shirt, forging
idioms so far beyond your time, praise be,

Rowley. Do you sleep soundly in the divine
abattoir of claustrophobic fibbery? Bedeviled,

be-nailed into the buttress of a sagging nave: this,
the shadow road to reality, carted like a sack

of Murphys o'er a bridge of whispers. Sip hard
ginger from the tin; be praised, as all great pewterers

aspire to the heights of goldsmiths to gild
our lips with lead. Dear dyspeptic Rowley, compose

thyself. To rise from the imaginary to what
we are or pretend—here in what

we say, our fricatives go to seed in a whiff
to shroud the lily field in walking onions.

By St George's Hill

1.

Having lost the belief of youth that death
will let me pass, I stalk secrets

inside a senseless birth, a savoury stuffed
with beef and scripture. In Mother's

kitchen, knives like a feathered brigade
line the wall, a side of pork laid darkly

'cross the planks—we've the shadow
of St George's Hill to make

black pudding, thickened with a blood
of thanks. My morning hungry for tomorrow,

I think what havoc I might spin for a mouldering
wheel of cheddar. How

to imagine a better day over a cockcrow
bowl of paste, then carry on toasting

2.

to our youth. We have nothing
but the finest, Tom. Just

yesterday I visited a friend's farm, the choir
of milking machines calmed

the heifers—those aluminum angels labour
for nothing but our succour, our cream

white clothes, poured from a vat
of chemicals—no sheep

need shearing. And please, Tom, take
care to shoo them from the feed bins else

they chew until their stomachs burst. Whether your
world or this, our days are a simple

succotash—we'll be remembered for
how we succumbed to what we didn't say.

In the Chase Near Portishead

Those days of foxglove and sea holly, Polly
played the chase. We picnicked

out near Portishead where, before the edging
pine of Savermake, we exchanged provisional

vows. That afternoon sullen Gritstones
blessed us, our every whim was music

made with sticks and rocks, our pleasures
blunt. That evening she wore a Bible 'tween

her pretties. Then chanced a gentleman
to take his lunch upon her hope chest

linen for ravishment by pretty
jests. Still, I relish that heart's blood

pudding, as if beauty were a morsel
nurtured in the gut for all my days of hunger.

Shadow of the Enlightenment

Why, by wretched arsenic—the body a shriveling
salted beetle—couldn't you

wait to cross the bridge above the granite
stairs that climb the thicket into Leigh

Woods where, like furrows of poppies,
stigmata grew in the dank

hope above ambitious leaves? All the burnings
of the Enlightenment still hurtle through space, dim

shimmer of a baffling planet—isn't that
what Science says to what's hidden inside the Poet's

Wing of the London Smallpox
Hospital? Tom, did your divine

beings wear surgical masks over oiled
goatees to execute their fruitless miracles?

Eclogue the Nth

This morning the landlord's bastard pilfers
my crusts, creeps into my dreams

disguised as a Christ of corn. Polly, that
heifer of hell's a brutal Beatrice, her love a swollen

wound suffered in Beelzebub's satin
daybed clouded by laments. The wagtail pours

her *spiritus fermenti* to soothe my wretchedness—all
the more dipping, Miss Rumsey, to the man

with a farthing. Under her bumpy bustle, a rose
furred Medusa swallows whole

the hedgehogs she calls ex
lovers. Easy to love self-pity. Easy to learn

the steps of the hopping dance's utilitarian
touch and heave-ho hallelujah.

Indecision

Along the turn where the Avon falters
back toward Brislington, and hand-smoothed

fieldstone agrees with its decisions,
I stalk a weakening current, a mirror

to wandering, tracing faint verse
into sediment just

below whitewater. In a cloudburst, a shepherd
braves a hailstorm with his flock

and collie, solid as a stand of oak. Lightning
probes a nearby hill, then searches

for a farmhouse as I turn
back from river's edge, and take

refuge beneath a granite outcropping,
indistinguishable from my flock.

Impromptu Portraits, Early Spring

1.

Wherein my father painted his own eternity
box in mums, I seek love

in blossoms. My mother believes in her
poverty, cross-stitching with the needle

of providence an unfinished
arabesque. Like farmers who till dust beneath

a miserly welkin, we choke the air
dead souls exhale. By ale and ignorance,

we kiss sour flesh, and from
our pantries pluck weevils fat as bishops

to bless our sawdust bread. Welcome, brother
cockroach, seeking counsel among

crumbs. Tom, are they not prophets
from our far promise? Yea, it's fair

2.

to dream of Spain, proclaim
our genius, as the penniless

chirurgeon plumps our humours with Sunday
leeches and pumps

back in with ale. From a seaside
pub, a ruined man staggers to retch

'longside the haberdasher of souls, who
never yields on price

to acquire by the yard. We can
measure depths above

and down, seahorse lucky in the drowning
wave, recalled in the frigate

wake that follows, returning all to their
misremembered grace.

Anatomy of the Soul

Exhausted from a day's labour smudging
mistakes from encyclopedic ledgers, might

you miss it, transcendent in an alley
off Charing Cross, translucent in oil

light? Glassy organs flood with crystal
blood driven by heartache

but for the moon's edge dulled
pink as a pig knuckle. Just shy

of the supernatural in a bedroom's
last word, all flesh and every

item of furniture's brought
back to the world by her painted

toes—love and blood of an inside
river burning all the way down.

Tom's Inheritance

We shout and skip along a trickle, some
graves and henges past St Redcliffe, where

the fat sexton paws dripping
sausage and French kale

pie atop a gravestone over
which his hairless legs dangle

alabaster toes like biscuits. A weathervane's
copper cock points toward

unfed graves overflowing
with mud I set aside for you and your fellow

poorhouse dreamers, heirs to hard
earth, as your mum and sis by whale oil wick

mend the wealthy moneymonger's
pantaloons and set broad the bone bustier of his witch.

Port of Call

Study close the articles of the Murder Act—
the menu of tiny human souls, unsteady

deckhands of Leviathan—the weather
of late gives naught

but refusal—clouds weave, wigless
as retiring lords. Larks lose themselves

in the air. At Customs House, a roundhead
slaver loads a case of gin

as comfort for the triangular
tour, staggers down the dock

to the Bristol Wharf Coach
& Horses Pub where accounts

settle, lumpy and reeking
of rancid beef in a canvas sack. Heed ye well.

The Old Road to London

Let nothing but the promise of lilies
and songs of shag-bag shepherds cloud

your way. You've come to make your way, Dearest
Tom—my west a mirror to your east. Off

Bristol, past fermenting granaries
that pitch their fields toward

Patchway and Portishead, askance
off Westbury on Trym, fluxed from the River

Avon longwise toward Avonmouth to devour
sunlit leaves of Leigh Woods and Abbots

Leigh, toward Sheepway and Pill—follow
the unwinding Thames, hoist your knapsack

as you leave Spike Island to its sublime
loneliness, eastward to London.

Sadness of the Carriage

Before twilight, the matron giving off
a rotting orchid malodor stepped

up into the cabin, blotting the Cheltenham
sunset that flared behind another

passenger, who turned a translucent
onionskin. Facing me and dressed

in black, he'd nearly given up his journey, already
disembarked from his body, acquired

from a Fitzrovia counting house. Nearly there, even
the horses are the worse. When I step

out into the depot's silence, will
my friend recognise—nearly invisible behind

my book-heavy valise, and the hell of this
life engraved into my skin—me?

III

Had I the gifts of wealth and luxury shar'd,
Not poor and mean, *Walpole*! thou hadst not dar'd
Thus to insult. But I shall live and stand
By *Rowley's* side, when thou art dead and damn'd.

    —Thomas Chatterton, from "To Horace Walpole,"
      July 1769

1770, London

Midsummer we'll savour a blackbird pie, crusted
with bitter herbs for the fly-happy banquet

of suffering. We can nick our daily
from the shopkeepers on Shakespeare's

Row sweeping the commons, who can't spare
a nod. After a night feeding the Puss

and Mew, we're wakened by the jennies groaning
over crushed glass that crusts the ruffled

blouse factory walls off St Pancras. Spindles
rattle cobblestone into our soles

as we traipse to the Pickled
Griffon, abreast of amateur dandies fresh

from haberdashers, wigs lustrous
as chandeliers to light the faces of the factory dead.

Sidewalk Screevers

Propped against London Bridge in whatever midday
shade they find, where you, fellow traveler, might

hunker, like the wise fly of August that expires
overnight, to sell your wares. A few

pennies for a catchy saw; a shilling, Good
Sir, for a rhyme? A sketch, perhaps, of Willie

Pitt the Younger's prat shiny
as a Tory cheek, forehead bowed

as a brigantine low with spice for Hogarth's
kitchen? A pure one—young as Aphrodite's

teat—has sketched a Madonna to trample till she's mopped
away at daybreak. Beside her, fingers twisted like a Belgrave

shrub, an old hand chalks a winding
staircase to the king of an army of locusts.

Thomas Seeks a Patron, or Lunch

To hell with Poesy, Tom, there's no
money in't—the famous

are famous for their cruelty. Didn't Walpole—quill
celebrated as a mule's fluffed

tail—send you packing? How could the Great
Man not see that Rowley breathed as much

as he? All flesh defined by the fancy of ha'penny
atoms, does imagination not, exhaling,

grieve its creations and swoon in the same
bordellos as the flesh? Let the curtal

friars share their psalms and stupors: that
summer, gut empty, you couldn't rouse

a syllable, the smoke of ghosts rising above
your pen—a silence of regrets instead of pleas.

For the Legacy of Mister Walpole

To ride the hermaphrodite horse—by birthright
you walk idyllic hedgerows and climb

the tower to break the bread of your mouldy
heart. To be Sir Robert's son, your burden

to somehow splash out four-thousand
per year. How to fit the daily leisures born

to the Usher of the Exchequer
and Comptroller of the Pipe? Shall you

author some turmoil of this or that, true
sycophant of Mary—composer of *Fashionable*

Friends—Berry? Must thou humour the pimply
angst of all adolescent ambition? Now, off

to Twickenham, on your pony to tend
the posies withered on Strawberry Hill!

Grub Street Parties

Shall we ruin an evening's West End
bash with drunken verse of heaving

melancholy, or crash a hell club orgy? Wander
this empty circus back to our dead

air garret, sober enough to stagger
into morning? Let's choke another quick

caesura and from our window stalk the motley
resurrectionists as they search for volunteers

below on Brooke Street, wagon heavy
with surrendered bodies as they clatter toward the all

night office of the Company of Barber Surgeons. Let us
lie low lest our own immortality, by the physician's curious

pego, be anatomised. If we listen, we'll hear the hiss
of souls released to heaven by the pound.

Epistle to the Hangman's Mistress

Dear Most Excellent Madame, consort to the King's
duly appointed murderer, the rope's

incandescent for a rainy gallows
feast on Execution Dock, his rough

grasp smoothed by years of ragged hemp. This
life's not just for the hard stipend of Newgate

wages to buy what love and death may sell—yea,
to smell the pink that once adorned today's neck

du jour. You may gloat over one whose spine's
been boned by rope—newborn to loss like Jesus

to disbelief. To the two-face jakes now
to primp till he staggers home to caress your neck

above the trap door, pried
wide to peer into the deep beneath your shimmer.

The Unexpurgated

To read your ridicule of the Reverend
Alexander Catcott's expressive—yet subtle—

tallywacker, no longer must we stoop
downcast in a backroom closet of the British

Museum, hidden from Creation. Held
here in our time, Thomas, idle

and incurious, where smut procreates
imaginary offspring, sprouting among

toadstools in a glooming woodlot, we suffer
gladly our own reputations. All

of us will read what's true enough and enter
the same eternity, whose old dimensions hide

their burn like bricks warming at the foot of a bed
where the carnal sleep with the unborn.

On the Resurgence of Plague in Moscow

The news comes to London of the Great
Mortality in Moscow, reminder of our

smugness. A mother discarded on the death-cart
overnight, children heaped onto a passing

bier at daybreak. The Great Emptiness comes
to collect our human taxes, the Blue

Sickness drains into the bluest sea, leaving our
scuttles stacked in tiers like a ship's

cargo for an alien voyage. Surely
the end is near, yet surely not—small

endings come a thousand times
a day. I'll leave space here for you, reader,

to chronicle your fate, which you must jot
quickly while struck by lightning lightning lightning.

Against the Princess of Wales, Augusta of Saxe-Gotha

May John Wilkes—sulfurous gadfly—be
the last to grunt upon your tiara, a slop

pot filched from the bath at St
Cross Almshouse. May your skin

shuffle there threadbare to greet your God
bareheaded. I wish you served in golden

chantries as you prostrate to the mob, mud
flecked mane fanned to hide your boiled

pudding, gas puffed wig excited to battle
swans that glide the debtor castle

moat. May you hire the solicitor of Pigs'
Law, your lech'rous suitors frightened

off, pointed ears flushed and perked to bask
by the bonfire of your pinchfist seductions.

John Wilkes Makes His Case

An ugly man's skin may be deep, his heart
a Queensland sundew for the poor, his blood

a tonic for injustice or syrup to seize
a royal cramp. Does a spirit crackle

in the fire of the King's speech, his neck
saved by god's tourniquet? Hold

a seat at the banquet where the insolent
speak against the gin-palsied fist

that aims to slit thy free-thinking throat. Stop
a moment, now, and ponder America,

ignorant of all that's come before, and still
make way for fresh-faced tyrants, proclaimed

with greasy fingertips inked
in the oil of prophets for hire.

On Hogarth's *The Bruiser*

Where Charlie Churchill found no peace, the man's
man of words, late master of the West Side's best

hellfire club and political privy, what
may John Wilkes, a last free man, scratch into his

pamphlet? Hogarth's loyal pug, Trump, can
piddle in the King's courtroom, his plug

tail o' musk airy as your hefty
feather. Now, the dogs upon us, these true

believers know our scent. Furious
prophets pitched in acid, pressed

into the service of debtor ghosts, we
have our say as we follow the angle

of a blunt-head club, wielded by a vellum
soul who ponders the smudge that marks our edge.

The Philosopher's Walk

Rogering mushy peas in this public
house of rogues, we'll shovel the gap with a few

pints of cunning, mesmerised by shadows
cast from the Enlightenment. Hacked

twain, Truth's offspring journey from the begotten,
hedge-whores borne upward into the worldly pink—

here in momentary perfection. Who
can stomach the wise? Reason teases with a raunchy

heel and toe. What's thinking but dumb luck, dim
as a noonday reading lamp? How many

for the speckled one to hold forth? Watch
now and listen to the thinker who speaks

of moderation, who heads our way on the King's
Road, stepping high to air his bollocks.

How to Give Up Poetry: A Broadside

Sleep in weeds flush with rodents; climb
the web of oaks to conspire

with an avaricious crow to wrest
a worm from the tree of would-be heaven. Interrogate

the page till snowlight clears our palate; then crack
the gut to catch what matters—if we lose

sleep to catch a feckless word, just figure it's worth
its weight in lust. Prove your mettle

at novelettes, or the stage perhaps to feed
a phrase to another's maw contorted in plagiarised

emotion, grease paint dripping
pale; to cease just give yourself

to life, patient as the carnivorous pitcher plant
that lies in wait so near the hive.

Chatterton Meets Rimbaud

Alone, fingers pressed to butcher board, a crimson
bandage wrapped 'cross

his brow to hold him here a moment
more, until like sails unfurled *Auntie, another*

please! To the public house, where *sale petit
Cagot* fondles another bulbous absinthe glass. Circling

till one espies the other, they follow the flowing
gowns of *la fée verte*, hallucinating

their merry way to Senegal. In Sahara heat, a frocked
buzzard from that burning heaven impersonates the gentle

nightingale of their youth. What shall
become of them—gun runners in the Sahel or back

home suicides? Shall they leap
hand-in-hand together?

IV

This is the last Will and Testament of me, Thomas Chatterton, of the city of Bristol; being sound in body, or it is the fault of my last surgeon: the soundness of my mind, the coroner and jury are to be the judges of, desiring them to take notice, that the most perfect masters of human nature in Bristol distinguish me by the title of the Mad Genius; therefore, if I do a mad action, it is comfortable to every action of my life, which all savoured of insanity.

To Mr. Burgum all my prosody and grammar, – likewise one moiety of my modesty; the other to any young lady who can prove without blushing that she wants that valuable commodity.

—Thomas Chatterton, from "Chatterton's Will," April 1770

Quick Note to Mother

At the coaching inn near Winterbourne, I write
how poetry will buy exotic

spices and rare ointments equal to the beauty
of my lines. Doubt no longer torments—how

the young, not by increments, may
pass beyond what can be learned, their lives

drawn by an inner
hand. In verse, I'll gather dragon fruit

and passionflowers, and bleed the spring
lamb spiced with mint. Mother please

tell Sister we'll save for her the giblet and greasy
neck, as when Father lived, to feast

upon what we may dream like famished
nurslings in the Cheapside of the afterlife.

Off *Gin Lane*, waltzing

fleas make their devotions to the primordial
copse of Tewkesbury's powdered

periwig, buoyed by an airy faith in
the fog that blankets patinated

headstones. Impossible figments once
ideas now congeal into flesh with

a taste for blood instead
of facts—hungry as Grub Street nibs they suckle

ink late into the work lamp dusk, without
patron or host, heartened with blue

ruin. You'd have ruled here, Tom, re
inventing us as if carving a haunch with blunt

intent, blood
browning on your spattered apron.

Mister Smart's Knowhow

That horrid spring of '52, indentured
to ghostwrite Satan's songbook, Mister

Chris rides his Phaeton 'round Finsbury
Circus to pocket one more prize. What praise might

humble the anointed? Even the Milkmaid Poet
Yearsley's happy *Stanzas of Woe* enshrine

her as resident demigoddess at Birdcage
Walk. And to the west, Twm o'r Nant

aka Tom o' the Dingle's mystery
play of vinegar'd elderberry entertains

a West End party for the lately feted
while Chatterton's dropped into an unmarked

slot in Shoe Lane Workhouse Cemetery, not a paid
mourner or union ghoul to bleed his pockets.

To Be Human

Tides, Thomas, inside the body betray
our spine. A rigid schooner transports

us—a simple membrane to seal the drifting
shapes that squirm like ants into an eternity

of amber. How to fathom such until
our hearts blow their red

doors open? What it is
to be—our blood a treacle

salted with alphabets to contort
into legend on the tongues of knaves,

poets, and footmen—guilt inbred as a little
one knows to suck, how the female

worker bee knows honeycomb and when
to dispense the one sting it's given.

A Last August

In cruelest London where the mail comes twice and ten
a day, the streets loud with horses, windows

rattle with hooves on cobble, the stench
of horseshit shovelled high as the aspiring vicar's

coach house. Flies ply
our faces with an angel's urgency

who's burnt her wings
to cinders. In this heat, e'en the Brixton

whores won't come to your
Brooke Street attic, won't swive

for verses. You choose this August to give it up
for revolution. We're so close to free, yet

so far from compromise—the heart's a sack
to suffocate a nervous hare.

Dear Thomas

Couldn't America be the father
you lost, the mother you failed? America, whose

philosophers are bookkeepers,
whose great thinkers lure acolytes

with clickbait. In a week you'll master
code and make the bangers and mash to buy

the games you'll need to patter flash
the melancholy. If you sail around

the cape and meet me at the Golden Gate,
chain link will keep us from the bluest

water. We'll float on that painted sunset, just
beyond the reach of doubt. Thomas, be

patient, save your pence, and stow away on the first
three-master to the New World, or the next.

Every Day a Little Suicide

This grammar school kid put
a shotgun in his mouth and pulled

the trigger with his toe. What did he
foresee he might someday be, the bead

on the family blunderbuss, a moist
ball of opium? From nine storeys up, I spot seven

church steeples along the Baghdad
by the Bay skyline—there, beside the joint

with the best pho, St Patrick's in the shadow of the new
Salesforce spire. At lunch, I pull a volume

from my backpack and sniff some lines before I start
this guide on how to knock

together a cloud. No one here, Thomas,
hurries. No one dies for truth. No one.

From Childhood

Now freed from a tongue-tied scurvy, I dream
of the lime groves of Temple Gardens, where

a death rattle's nothing more than a gypsy
dance. Fate's so easily distracted by

simple temptation. I know here
in the Great Wen, the doors of this hovel

will never let me pass. My childhood
relics arranged on the bed, this scrabble

of winter starves the heart. Maggots, nearly
cured by fermenting bitters, perform

their nightly circus. Though I had a morning
caller, I marked time until the footfalls

vanished—to go on fathoming
myself the first and last of my kind.

Worlds Betwixt

How, Tom, could you not yearn, among browning
tomes and an unfinished sun that dips

into an unfished sea, nothing between
you and there but a monstrous

will to disappear? Like an allemande stuck
in your head you hear it as you work

through the furious weather of your twilit
garret overlooking the roofs that

jut from the birthplace of sadness. What
to become but what you despise? One last

carriage cruise through Piccadilly: early
bird tarts saunter before an August

sundown blur, half dressed
by feathers of indolent swans.

A Visit to Thomas Cross, Apothecary

Arsenic, laudanum, clap, or pox? We
accommodate. Another jar of Dover's

powder, please, good for washing hooves
or to clear the mind—we can board the early

carriage to a forgotten Arcadia, where the hides
of blackened horses smolder on rooftops

from colliery chimneys. Here's a sonnet
for a pork pie, please, a hatchet

for a tankard. Here's an expletive
to express affection, a half pence

for my fortune. Don't forget love's phantom slips
its shade into the careless mouth: we need

no spoon for such hunger, the Spanish
itch nor Bible to parse the human error.

In Which Thomas Propositions an Angel

She haunts the burned-down barn, this
milkmaid who so despised the sour

air—sleepwalking from her new
life as shop girl in the gilded city. Tell her

you believe her, that the wheel
of heaven's invented a thousand times a day. As you lie

in the haystack offering pleasant
reckonings, beware. The eternal unrequited's

fickle as you make your way beneath her immaculate
aprons—she has time to spare while you,

old friend, have none after a night
warm beside the embers that consummate

the spirit; ebbing now, she returns to duly tug
the pure and flaxen, as on any day's fair passing.

Wherein Old Tom, Bent with Age, Imagines

Sit here and conjure what
your life might have been. A sip of English

craft to steady—now see yourself not
a glimmer of stone, but a grizzled

man of words, as book-smart ladies listen,
aflutter with your magnum

opus. The unwritten, like a London
fog hangs on dang'rous mews, reveals

fingers of a phantom limb to read
the secret face in the what-if crypt, where you

suffer the eternal doddering of Horace
the Lesser, who grasps your ankles

as you raise your ink-stained fingers above
your head, ready to ascend.

The Resurrection of Thomas Chatterton

If you could be shocked back from eternal
muck—prodigal returned, brother of Shelley's

righteous creature—heaven's maelstrom raging
above Romantic topcoats and the twitching

frogs of Galvani, you mayst still
dream a child's dream. Now, as you sleep,

the charwoman with the medicated
face of a retired jade scrubs the brick

fireplace and empties the pot where
you heaved last night. An old English

word neither of us can recollect bubbles
like hard cider on the tongue. We slouch

in firelight, and sweet Mary recites
her pregnant prose as you, a newborn monster, rise.

EPILOGUE

Farewell, ye guzzling aldermanic fools,
By nature fitted for Corruption's tools!
I go to where celestial anthems swell;
But you, when you depart, will sink to Hell.
Farewell, my Mother! Cease, my anguish'd soul,
Nor let Distraction's billows o'er me roll!
Have mercy, Heaven! when here I cease to live,
And this last act of wretchedness forgive.

    —Thomas Chatterton, from "Chatterton's
      Last Verses," August 1770

At Chatterton's Café, Redcliffe Way

Museum's closed 15 years, where your teenage
quill leans from a green glass inkwell on your

writing desk behind a velvet
rope. The family home a coffee bar, your

portrait hangs above the white chalked
menu: cucumber sandwich, latte five quid half

a nicker. Out on Redcliffe, a woman twice
your age speed walks—headphones up, eyes

straight—toward Temple Meads to a job
at the science park. In a corner, a sprite loiters

on his mobi to make a few last gestures in World
of Warcraft, brighter than window light, till

heading to his gaming job where, under an angel
misting invented air, he'll linger his hours away.

NOTES

Page 3, Cabinet of Wonders
    Whisk and swabbers: 18th-century English card game.

Page 14, Of the Immaculate Father
    William Canynge: Father-figure invented by Chatterton, his own father having died before he was born.

Page 15, Eighteenth-Century Pastimes
    Ruff-and-honours: 18th-century English card game.

Page 17, Mystery Play
    Jacob's ladder and battledore: English children's games.

Page 23, In which we introduce Friar Rowley, priest, nay poet
    Friar Rowley: 15th-century priest-poet invented by Chatterton.
    "An Excelente Balade of Charitie": Poem written in the persona of the invented priest-poet Thomas Rowley.
    Walpole: Horace Walpole, major literary figure of the time, to whom Chatterton sent his invented manuscript. At first, Walpole believed it to be authentic, but later, when Chatterton sent additional work, saw through the farce.
    Bottle and glass: Cockney rhyming slang for "ass."

Page 24, Essay on Composition
    William Dugdale, Liz Cooper's *Muses Library*, Samuel Daniel: Books and authors in the library at Chatterton's home that, along with Chaucer's *Canterbury Tales*, Chatterton used as source material to invent the Rowley poems.

Page 25, The Word of Friar Rowley Ripens, Briefly, into Flesh
    Murphys: Irish potatoes.
    Pewterers: Pewter goods were a major product produced in Bristol.

Page 28, In the Chase Near Portishead
    Polly: Polly Rumsey, love interest of Chatterton, who spurned him for a more affluent prospect.

Page 36, Port of Call

    Murder Act: The Murder Act of 1752 called for the bodies of murderers to be made available for dissection by anatomists to dissuade resurrectionists from exhuming bodies from cemeteries.

    Leviathan: Thomas Hobbes argued that the greedy passions of humanity form the beast Leviathan and must be controlled by government.

    Roundhead: Puritan, who wore hair closely cropped.

    Triangular tour: The triangular trade, a shipping route for transporting slaves and sugar, included the Caribbean, West Africa, and the Port of Bristol.

    Coach & Horses: Pub on the Bristol Wharf where the Royal Navy and ship owners collected drunks and pressed them into sea duty.

Page 37, The Old Road to London

    Shag-bag: Sneaky man without spirit.

Page 41, 1770, London

    Puss and Mew: Coin-operated machine in the shape of a cat to dispense gin, circumventing the Gin Act.

Page 42, Sidewalk Screevers

    Prat: Buttocks.

Page 43, Thomas Seeks a Patron, or Lunch

    Curtal friar: Friar who acted as a porter at a monastery gate.

Page 44, For the Legacy of Mister Walpole

    Usher of the Exchequer and Comptroller of the Pipe: Hereditary positions held by Walpole that provided him a substantial income.

    Mary Berry: Author of the play *Fashionable Friends*, which closed after three performances.

    Strawberry Hill: Walpole's Gothic Revival villa in London.

Page 45, Grub Street Parties

    Grub Street: District in London near flophouses and brothels, inhabited by hack writers, failed poets, and lower-rung publishing houses.

Resurrectionists: Body snatchers, who exhumed cadavers from fresh graves and sold them to anatomists for dissection.

Company of Barber Surgeons: Association of surgeons formed to regulate practices, such as how many executed convicts may be dissected in public per year.

Pego: Penis.

Page 46, Epistle to the Hangman's Mistress

Newgate: London prison so dismal that 30 prisoners died there each year and physicians often refused to enter.

Jakes: Toilet.

Page 47, The Unexpurgated

Alexander Catcott: Target of Chatterton's satirical poem "Epistle to the Reverend Mr. Catcott."

Tallywacker: Penis.

Backroom closet of the British Museum: For decades, poems by Chatterton that were considered obscene could only be read by special request behind a barrier in the British Museum.

Page 49, Against the Princess of Wales, Augusta of Saxe-Gotha

John Wilkes: Revolutionary Chatterton wanted to join in London. Wilkes was a notorious figure, once reciting in parliament an obscene poem ridiculing another member.

St Cross Almshouse: Hospital of St Cross and Almshouse of Noble Poverty.

Page 50, John Wilkes Makes His Case

Queensland sundew: Carnivorous plant in Australia.

Page 51, On Hogarth's The Bruiser

The Bruiser: Engraving that caricatures the poet Charles Churchill, a compatriot of John Wilkes, in response to Churchill's *Epistle to William Hogarth*, a personal attack on Hogarth.

Hellfire club: Clubs for English and Irish gentlemen who wanted to participate in activities unacceptable to society.

Trump: Hogarth's dog, a pug, depicted in *The Bruiser* urinating on Churchill's book, *Epistle to William Hogarth*.

Page 52, The Philosopher's Walk
>Hedge-whore: Itinerant prostitute who plied her trade in the "hedges."
>Bollocks: Testicles.

Page 54, Chatterton Meets Rimbaud
>Senegal: Both Chatterton and Rimbaud had their African periods. Rimbaud abandoned poetry to run guns in northern Africa; Chatterton wrote a set of antislavery poems, the *African Eclogues*.
>*Sale petit Cagot*: Rimbaud's schoolyard nickname.
>*La fée verte*: Green fairy, absinthe.

Page 58, Off Gin Lane, waltzing
>*Gin Lane*: Etching by Hogarth depicting a scene of depraved and drunken Londoners.
>Periwig: White wig worn by fashionable men.

Page 59, Mister Smart's Knowhow
>Mister Smart: Christopher Smart began his career on Grub Street, eventually becoming a successful and celebrated poet.
>Phaeton: Open carriage popular with the European sporty set.
>Yearsley: Working class poet Ann Yearsley, buried at Bristol's Birdcage Walk, whose *Stanzas of Woe* and other works were very popular.
>Twm o'r Nant aka Tom o' the Dingle: Pen names of Welsh poet Thomas Edwards.

Page 62, Dear Thomas
>Bangers and mash: Cockney rhyming slang for money.
>Patter flash: Language used by thieves and pickpockets to communicate unnoticed by their marks.

Page 66, A Visit to Thomas Cross, Apothecary
>Arsenic, laudanum, clap, or pox: Some have speculated that Chatterton may have contracted syphilis; he died by taking the arsenic provided by Thomas Cross, a local apothecary. Whether his death was suicide or an accidental overdose is uncertain.

Dover's powder: Medicine made partly of opium that was a pain reliever and also caused perspiration to reduce fever, developed by Thomas Dover, ex-buccaneer, of Bristol.
Spanish itch: Syphilis.

Page 69, *The Resurrection of Thomas Chatterton*

Galvani: Luigi Galvani's early experiments in reanimation—applying electricity to dead frogs causing their legs to move—and of later scientists who applied electricity to executed convicts were a scientific inspiration for Mary Shelly's *Frankenstein*.

AFTERWORD

In 1762, at the age of ten, a Bristol schoolboy named Thomas Chatterton (1752–1770) told his elder sister Mary: "my name will live three hundred years." Living in poverty and supported only by his mother Sarah's meagre earnings as a seamstress–his father having died two months before his birth–the scope of young Thomas's ambition was only matched by the enormity of his imagination.

In the end, Chatterton was vindicated. His name has indeed lived on–though his reputation has undergone many transformations since his untimely death in 1770 at the age of 17. In forging one of English literature's shortest, most controversial, and most outrageous careers Chatterton, as Peter Ackroyd says in his preface to *Thomas Chatterton and Romantic Culture* (1999), "has survived a variety of literary incarnations ranging from Augustan fraudster to Romantic icon and post-modern avatar." Chatterton has lived on as a spectre, haunting and inspiring Romantic poets, Pre-Raphaelite painters, and postmodern novelists.

Chatterton's greatest influence was upon the generation of Romantic poets that flourished in the late eighteenth and early nineteenth centuries. Samuel Taylor Coleridge's first published poem was "On the Death of Thomas Chatterton" (1790) whilst Chatterton's death was commemorated in the forty-fifth stanza of Percy Bysshe Shelley's *Adonais* (1821). In his "Resolution and Independence," published in *Poems in Two Volumes* (1807), William Wordsworth bestowed the immortal moniker of "the marvellous Boy" on a poet whose life and works also profoundly influenced William Blake, John Keats, and Lord Byron.

George Rawlins's *Cheapside Afterlife* is a collection of sonnets reimagining Chatterton's life: the latest poetic tribute to Chatterton. Part epitaph, part elegy, part panegyric, Rawlins's powerful and well-crafted sequence retells Chatterton's story with the wit, lyricism, and invention appropriate for an homage to English poetry's most tragic figure. It begins by setting out its wares: "Cabinet of Wonders" invokes an Enlightenment-themed "cover band" and peddles its "objects of curiosity" by asking impishly: "Why/not jitterbug the Age of Reason?"

In "A Jot of Blood," we see images of "Redcliffe's belfry" (near Chatterton's birthplace) as well as the father Chatterton never met, who "clash[es] with heaven" as his mother sews, huddled next to a fire. Rawlins's Chatterton looms into view for the first time with "expectations to make/my mark," vowing "I am who cannot/be" and urging the reader to "disbelieve this/world, invent what's not, to spice our/humdrum tongue." Rawlins's collection takes up, as Chatterton did, a fascination with the relationship between reality and fiction—what Donald S. Taylor in his book *Thomas Chatterton's Art* (1979) called Chatterton's "experiments in imagined history."

After a difficult start to his education, Chatterton developed a precocious intellect and prodigious reading habit, frequently lending books from circulating libraries. His teacher at Colston's School said he was "very fond of reading black letter print particularly old Poetry" but Chatterton did not, according to William Henry Ireland (another famous forger) in his *Confessions*, "confine himself to any particular head, but perused promiscuously works on religion, history, biography, poetry, heraldry—and, in short, the most abstruse treatises on every subject." James Thistlethwaite, in an account printed in J. Milles's 1782 edition of Chatterton's *Poems*, remembered his friend's eclectic reading:

> One day he might be found busily employed in the study of Heraldry and English Antiquities [...]. [T]he next, discovered him deeply engaged, confounded, and perplexed, amidst the subtleties of metaphysical disquisition, or lost and bewildered in the abstruse labyrinth of mathematical researches.

Chatterton divulged to Thistlethwaite his desire to become a poet, promising that if he failed he would instead pretend to a career as a "Methodist preacher" since "Credulity is as potent a deity as ever, and a new sect may easily be devised." A local apothecary would later recall that "he loved talking about religion and to argue against Christianity."

Accordingly, Rawlins imagines Chatterton pondering the great scientific works of his age. In "Essay on Knowledge," we are urged to consider "What lesson of reason could/be mastered without tasting arsenic of the apple/seed?" and "With what calculus did Leibniz measure the variable/slope of suffering?" Chatterton's depression was well known. His boss, John Lambert, according to Chatterton's early biographer George Gregory, remarked on his employee's "gloomy temper." According to his sister, Chatterton suffered frequent "melancholy fits." The grinding poverty of the family's early days in Bristol is vividly evoked by Rawlins in images of "Hunger, that ingratiating parasite" and "leper's bread malformed on long/spare tables." "At Colston Hospital School" revisits Chatterton's education: "Matins of the bum brushers teach/us to sleep, bind our scalps as if tonsured by/the firmament to unrelenting ignorance," he says, before asking: "won't we/schoolboys one day drift above bluebell/automatons[?]"

This is a formative moment in Chatterton's career and Rawlins is right to emphasise it. Chatterton was enchanted by medieval history at Colston School, where the boys wore Tudor-style bluecoats and were made to wear their hair tonsured like monks. Yet his father's legacy was also key. Thomas Chatterton senior was the former writing master of St Mary Redcliffe School and an amateur antiquarian who collected medieval charters, muniments, and coins, and possessed a sizable library of over 150 books. After school, Chatterton secured an apprenticeship as a legal scrivener. Yet with little to do during his 12-hour shift, he spent his time instead researching medieval England and exploring his father's collections.

It was at this time, when Chatterton was still just 13 or 14, that he invented "Thomas Rowley," a fifteenth-century Bristol monk, described by Chatterton in a footnote to his "The Ryse of Peyncteynge, yn Englande" (1769) as "a Secular Priest of St. John's, in this City. [H]is Merit as a Biographer, Historiographer is great, as a Poet still greater: some of his Pieces would do honour to [Alexander] Pope." Already, Chatterton was aiming high. Inhabiting the persona, Chatterton began to compose poems, plays, letters, and antiquarian treatises in Rowley's name.

In "Southwark Broadside," Rawlins muses that "Truth's serrated—slick and fickle bedfellow of/fibs—companion to ash." This masterful image recalls Chatterton's murky imaginative experiments in creating his Rowley fakes. John Rudhall, an apprentice apothecary in Bristol, helped (or witnessed) Chatterton ageing forged manuscripts by staining them with yellow ochre, soot, and ash and holding them over a candle or fire to char the vellum. In Rawlins's vision, we are made complicit in Chatterton's forgeries: the reader is his "closest conspirator," pulled along for the ride as we "follow the wandering screed." As Nick Groom, one of the foremost Chatterton scholars, says in his account of Chatterton's life published in the *Oxford Dictionary of National Biography*: "It was literary forgery, but forgery in the fullest sense of the word: these were crafted textual artefacts—original antique verse often transcribed in a crabbed and ancient calligraphy in aged ink on old vellum, frequently illuminated with naïve heraldic sketches and architectural cartoons." It begs the question, Groom points out in *Chatterton and Romantic Culture*: "Were they really forgeries?" or "Were they a new form of fiction?"

Rawlins picks up this enigmatic thread as he wonderfully imagines the genesis of Chatterton's Rowley in "For the Green Man": "From this valley's heartless plenty, invent a life that/should have been. Free him from his imaginary/grave. Call him *Rowley*." He then beautifully concocts an image of Chatterton inventing Rowley as if he were God creating Adam, with ingredients inspired by the Weird Sisters' "hell-broth" in Shakespeare's *Macbeth* (c.1603) (4.1.19): "For his/loblolly, a celestial-spiced clod; a sprig/of fur clipped from a back alley puss/to warm his pointer."

Rawlins also vividly evokes the spaces of the young Chatterton's world in South West England: "Like limestone priests the Bristol/cliffs shed their burdens beneath/ a deadpan heaven." *Cheapside Afterlife* charts Rawlins's own journey through Chatterton: he speaks to the departed poet sometimes as an encouraging friend, sometimes as an admonishing tutor. He occasionally betrays his exasperation with his mysterious charge: "I took back my college reading list," he says, "hid/from Tom behind a crispy *Tristram/Shandy*." Yet he finishes with a loving tribute, "At Chatterton's Café, Redcliffe Way," where "your teenage/quill leans from a green glass inkwell on your/writing desk behind a velvet/rope."

Throughout, Rawlins staunchly defends Chatterton's literary fakes: "Whose life is not most/invention?" he demands, asking pointedly: "is/this life bearable sans beauteous/fakery?" and scorning the "exactly-who-/they-are" as "stumbling/dreamers of their own disinvention." In Rawlins's evocative poetry, self-fabrication and self-fashioning by way of outrageous fictions and forgeries become the keys to authenticity. He takes aim at Horace Walpole in a grotesque, *Spitting Image*-esque vision: "Is not Walpole, simmering his/chunky giblets in a viscous/prose, more blanched spirit than flesh?" This recalls a key turning point in Chatterton's career. He wrote to Walpole on 25 March 1769 with "The Ryse of Peyncteynge," which was advertised as written by Rowley in 1469. Walpole, a keen antiquarian, was initially taken in. But when Chatterton revealed his poverty and Walpole consulted friends who suspected forgery, the plan was rumbled. Yet Chatterton was not cowed: he went on to publish more than fifty works in many literary, political, and historical journals under an array of pseudonyms. Indeed, Rawlins's collection is itself a hymn to Chatterton's defiant response to Walpole's rejection. "I think myself injured, sir," he wrote in July 1769, "and, did not you know my circumstances, you would not dare to treat me thus."

Chatterton is alleged to have written a poem attacking Walpole, later persuaded against sending it by his sister Mary. "Walpole," it begins, "I thought not I should ever see/So mean a Heart as thine has prov'd to be." "Say, didst thou ne'er indulge in such Deceit?/Who wrote Otranto?" These "Lines to Walpole" might be a forgery by Chatterton's biographer John Dix but they certainly shed light on the poet's clash with Walpole.

The first edition of *The Castle of Otranto* (1764) was marketed as "A Story. Translated by William Marshal, Gent. From the Original Italian of Onuphrio Muralto," supposedly a manuscript dating from 1529. After its runaway success, Walpole claimed authorship and the second edition duly bore his name along with the subtitle: *A Gothic Story*. The revelation led to Walpole being condemned as "false" and "preposterous" by the poet and clergyman John Langhorne on account of the deceit. The whole affair is curious when Walpole's extensive antiquarian credentials are taken into account. Walpole had attacked ministers in George III's government for their misreadings of medieval history and its relics, especially manuscripts. But given the liberties he himself took with "history," perhaps Walpole's anger was born of his shame that Chatterton held a mirror up to his own literary forgeries.

Rawlins's collection is itself a lyrical witness to Chatterton's bombastic project. "Essay on Composition" sees Rawlins prepare another recipe, this time a roll call of the ingredients of Chatterton's fictions, from Geoffrey Chaucer to Philip Sidney. "Sniff the Wife of Bath," he says, and:

> …Shake off some Samuel
>
> Daniel melodrama with a ménage of feminine
> endings, splash a double dactyl and brush
>
> the embers off the faery into your Earl
> Grey with a chastened Astrophel
>
> or Stella…

Rawlins lovingly traces and reimagines Chatterton's youth: a picnic "out near Portishead" and a trip to "Leigh/Woods where, like furrows of poppies,/stigmata grew in the dank/hope above ambitious leaves." These spaces are evoked with deft skill to render the topographical world of eighteenth-century Bristol and its bucolic surroundings, which recede from view as Chatterton's ambition leads him to take "The Old Road to London," not without a touch of melancholy, as Rawlins says: "as you leave Spike Island to its sublime/loneliness." In "Indecision," Rawlins fuses beautiful pastoral with a self-reflection on the wandering inherent in the process of writing poetry:

> Along the turn where the Avon falters
> back toward Brislington, and hand-smoothed
>
> fieldstone agrees with its decisions,
> I stalk a weakening current, a mirror
>
> to wandering, tracing faint verse
> into sediment just
>
> below whitewater. In a cloudburst, a shepherd
> braves a hailstorm with his flock
>
> and collie, solid as a stand of oak. Lightning
> probes a nearby hill, then searches
>
> for a farmhouse as I turn
> back from river's edge, and take
>
> refuge beneath a granite outcropping,
> indistinguishable from my flock.

"Quick Note to Mother" registers Chatterton's confidence that "poetry will buy exotic/spices and rare ointments equal to the beauty/of my lines." Indeed, the historical Chatterton enjoyed initial success with his creations. Chatterton's first published fabrication appeared in 1768 in *Felix Farley's Bristol Journal*: a "thirteenth-century" narrative of a Bristol bridge opening attributed to "Dunhelmus Bristoliensis." Chatterton "medievalized" the writing by copying the orthographic conventions used in Thomas Ruddiman's 1710 edition of Gavin Douglas's *Eneados* (1513), a translation into Scots of Virgil's *Aeneid*. Chatterton then deceived a local historian, William Barret, supplying him with forged manuscripts for his work-in-progress, *The*

History and Antiquities of the City of Bristol (1789). At this time, Chatterton joined a "Spouting Club," where young peers performed drama and poetry; it is here Chatterton developed the characteristic eighteenth-century taste for satire and mock-epic.

Chatterton then began to invent more characters around Rowley, contacting national publishers and eminent writers in an attempt to pass off his creations to a wider audience. Encouraged by his success, Chatterton finally moved to London in April 1770, writing back to his mother from Shoreditch: "Here I am, safe, and in high spirits." He apparently began to earn serious money, enough to buy presents for his family. He wrote to his sister in May 1770: "I employ my money now in fitting myself fashionably [...] and getting into good company." His nights were spent writing (he destroyed his early drafts in the morning), and he only drank water or tea and abstained from meat. He moved to Holborn, above a brothel where his rent was raised because he would not stop sleeping with the staff. In "Thomas Seeks a Patron, or Lunch," Rawlins chides "To hell with Poesy, Tom, there's no/money in't–the famous/are famous for their cruelty," warning ominously of "the smoke of ghosts rising above/your pen." The whole collection, indeed any re-telling of Chatterton's story, leads inexorably towards the night of 24 August 1770. Up in his cramped garret, Chatterton died from an overdose at 17 years of age.

It is popularly believed that Chatterton committed suicide due to his poverty and disappointment at being unable to sell his work. Indeed, this is the account Rawlins gives in the "Prologue" to *Cheapside Afterlife*. Chatterton's "gloomy" disposition was well-known but he in fact published seven pieces in June 1770 and had secured a book contract. He was loving life in the capital and his literary prospects appeared encouraging.

The poem "Will," which was written, according to Chatterton "bet[ween] 11 and 2 oClock Saturday in the utmost Distress of Mind" on April 14 1770, is a red herring that has often been misunderstood as a suicide note–despite being composed four months before his death. In fact, the tone is highly satirical throughout: it sarcastically gives notice of "my Death which will happen tomorrow night before 8 oClock being the feast of the resurrection" and ends claiming to have been "Executed in the presence of Omniscience," a quip in keeping with Chatterton's lifelong attention-seeking attacks on Christianity.

Chatterton may actually have been inspired by another mock will published by Samuel Derrick in *Town and Country Magazine*, itself a parody of the will of "Isaac Bickerstaff" published in *Tatler* in April 1709. The impulse behind the "Will" could even be traced back to his satirical compositions for the Spouting Club, but are in any case in concert with Chatterton's relentless urge to forge, invent, and mythologise his literary *personae*. Moreover, several key poems pointing towards suicide, including "Suicide Note" and "Chatterton's Last Verses," which contains the archetypal Romantic trope of "my anguish'd soul," are now suspected to be forgeries (of which Chatterton would no doubt have approved).

And so, for the vast majority of Chatterton scholars, the assumption that he committed suicide was called into serious question in the early 1970s. Groom notes that "His end was senseless and tragic, but despite the juggernaut of myth that began almost immediately to roll, obliterating history, this was no proto-Romantic suicide of a starving poet in a friendless garret, his genius cruelly unrecognized." Rather, "the devastating conclusion is that he died simply from unwisely mixing his venereal medicine with his recreational drugs." Several scientific studies analysing the liquid stains on Chatterton's memorandum book have confirmed that the death was most likely the result of an opiate overdose. One such study by Paul J. Gates and Michael L. Doble, published in the journal *Analyst* in 2020, concluded that "scientific evidence is overwhelming that the stain is the result of opiates, anything else is purely speculation, but the assertion that he committed suicide by arsenic poisoning should be, in the authors view, called into serious doubt."

Rawlins, like Coleridge, Wordsworth, Shelley, and the other Romantics, indulges and trades in the "juggernaut of myth" surrounding Chatterton's death: that he died of a broken heart, unfulfilled poetic ambition, and a deep depression. But this is no fatal detriment to *Cheapside Afterlife*. If anything, it elevates Rawlins's tribute to an exercise in "imagined history": the most fitting testimonial to Chatterton's fictions. Rawlins writes movingly of the "monstrous/will to disappear" and beautifully renders the "twilit/garret overlooking the roofs that/jut from the birthplace of sadness." The image of the rakish, licentious literary crook-turned-addict accidentally overdosing might lack the romance of the poet choosing death over obscurity. But Rawlins's collection, steeped in Chatterton's works and drawing on his subject's tenacious powers of invention, is a highly rewarding "jitterbug" through the poet's incredible career. In "Songe toe Ella," a Pindaric attributed to Rowley and composed in 1768, Chatterton says:

> O Thou or what remaines of thee
> Ella the Darlynge of Futuritie
> Let this my Songe bolde as thy Courage bee
> As everlastinge to Posterytie.

Cheapside Afterlife is a testament to Chatterton's outrageous ambition, a poetic memorial to Chatterton's "everlastinge [...] Posterytie." Rawlins's collection deserves to be read by anyone with an interest in Chatterton—or simply anyone who loves reading poetry crafted with true skill, humour, empathy, and learning.

—Josh Mcloughlin, *New Critique*

Josh Mcloughlin is a writer from Merseyside. He is the editor-in-chief of *New Critique*, a Wolfson Scholar in the Humanities at University College London, and he was shortlisted for the Jane Martin Poetry Prize (2019) and the International Awards for Art Criticism (2020). He writes for *The Times*, *The New Statesman*, *The Spectator*, *The Fence*, *The London Magazine*, and others.

Photo Credit:
Constance Rawlins

George Rawlins was born and raised in southeastern Ohio. He has a BA from Ohio University and an MFA from the University of California, Irvine. His work has appeared in *The Common, Illuminations, Nine Mile, Plainsongs, Sanskrit, Spinning Jenny*, and elsewhere. He lives in California.

Recent Books from Longleaf Press

Caravaggio's Kimono, Ken Fifer (2022 Longleaf Press Book Contest in Poetry Winner)
One Sky to the Next, Christopher Buckley (2021 Longleaf Press Book Contest in Poetry Co-winner)
O Body of Bliss, Janine Certo (2021 Longleaf Press Book Contest in Poetry Co-winner)
Down to Earth, Crystal Simone Smith
This Far from Perfect, Kate Fetherston
The Four Gentlemen and Their Footman, Roger Weingarten
Running Music, Crystal Simone Smith
Premature Elegy by Firelight, Roger Weingarten

www.ingramcontent.com/pod-product-compliance
Lightning Source LLC
Chambersburg PA
CBHW030557080526
44585CB00012B/405